To What
Miserable Wretches
Have I Been Born?

Also by Suzanne Weber (writing as Anita Liberty)

How to Heal the Hurt by Hating

How to Stay Bitter Through the Happiest Times of Your Life

The Center of the Universe (Yep, That'd Be Me)

To What **Miserable Wretches** Have I Been Born?

REVENGE POETRY
for BABIES and TODDLERS

Suzanne Weber

ATRIA BOOKS

New York   London   Toronto   Sydney   New Delhi

ATRIA BOOKS
A Division of Simon & Schuster, Inc.
1230 Avenue of the Americas
New York, NY 10020

First Atria Books hardcover edition April 2012

ATRIA B O O K S and colophon are trademarks of Simon & Schuster, Inc.

For information about special discounts for bulk purchases, please contact Simon & Schuster Special Sales at 1-866-506-1949 or business@simonandschuster.com.

The Simon & Schuster Speakers Bureau can bring authors to your live event. For more information or to book an event, contact the Simon & Schuster Speakers Bureau at 1-866-248-3049 or visit our website at www.simonspeakers.com.

Designed by Kyoko Watanabe

Manufactured in the United States of America

10 9 8 7 6 5 4 3 2 1

Library of Congress Cataloging-in-Publication Data

Weber, Suzanne, date.
To what miserable wretches have I been born? : revenge poetry for babies and toddlers / Suzanne Weber.—1st Atria Books hardcover ed.
    p. cm.
1. Parenting—Humor. 2. Infants—Care—Humor. 3. Toddlers—Humor. I. Title.
PN6231.P2W43 2012
811'.602—dc23   2011040946

ISBN 978-1-5011-1527-1

For my daughter, Julia, who has
been clearly expressing her point of view
since the moment she left my womb.
(Including the expectation that I dedicate
this book to her and that the dedication be
set in some sort of "fancy, scripty type.")

Contents

To What
Miserable Wretches
Have I Been Born?

Q: How do you breed contempt?

A: Have a baby.

Have You Thought This Through?

You do know I'm going to grow up,
get bigger,
more demanding,
participate more fully,
speak out more frequently,
don't you?

You wanted to have a baby.
but you probably didn't think much about having a toddler.
Or a child.
Or a 'tween.
Or a teenager.
Or an adult—
an adult who's gonna look at you, see only your flaws,
and have no qualms about outlining them to you in detail.
Didn't factor *that* into the equation, didja?
'Cause right now, you're looking at me
and my little,
chubby,
droolly,
toothless
face and thinking,
"This is the best decision I ever made."

Just wait.
You're in for it as soon as I have a vocabulary
large enough to make my criticisms effective.
Or at least as soon as I can
hold my neck up
without
support.

Where Are My Hands??!!??

I had hands.
I know I did.
I was born with them.
They were there this morning.
What have you done with them?!!??
For that matter, where are my arms?
Last thing I remember,
you lay me on a blanket
and just kept
wrapping
and twisting
and tucking
and tightening
and then
I had no hands.
Or arms.
Come to think of it, can't really see my legs or feet either.
And what exactly do you expect me to do in this position?
It's not really conducive to anything except lying here.
What if I just fall asleep like this?
You'd like that, wouldn't you?
Have this little limbless body fall asleep
so you wouldn't have to think
about my needs and attending to them.

You might as well have gotten yourself a houseplant.
Or a throw pillow.
Or a pet rock.
Whatever. Fine.
I'll sleep.
But only because
trying to do anything else
is
pointless.

Cry Guide

Cry #1: I'm hungry.
Cry #2: I'm tired.
Cry #3: I have a gas bubble.
Cry #4: My diaper needs to be changed.
Cry #5: Something scared me.
Cry #6: I have an ear infection.
Cry #7: I miss you.
Cry #8: I have diaper rash.
Cry #9: You took away something that was interesting to me.
Cry #10: You took away something that was comforting to me.
Cry #11: Life is stressing me out and I'm only in Year One.
Cry #12: Broccoli tastes like feet.
Cry #13: Daddy sang too loud.
Cry #14: You almost dropped me.
Cry #15: It's too dark.
Cry #16: It's too light.
Cry #17: I know you're never gonna let me get my nose pierced.
Cry #18: I'm understimulated.
Cry #19: I'm overstimulated.

Cry #20: I wish we had a dog.

Cry #21: I feel disappointed in you for reasons I'm having trouble articulating.

Cry #22: No more DAN ZANES!!

Cry #23: I poked myself in the eye.

Cry #24: Global warming.

Cry #25: No reason. I just like fuckin' with ya.

Some Changes Around Here

There are plenty of items
on which
you seem comfortable
splurging.

You couldn't resist the darling Bonpoint dress.
You loved the design of the Stokke crib.
You don't know what you'd do without your
Petunia Pickle Bottom diaper bag
and you're sure you'll use the
Béaba Babycook food maker
SOMEDAY
even though
TODAY
it's
STILL IN ITS BOX!

So what made you decide to skimp
when it came to picking up
a **WIPE WARMER** for me?
That's where you decide to draw the line?
That's the luxury item you forego?
That's not worth the money?

Oh, I can't tell you how fast you'd
get yourself and your American Express card over to
buybuy Baby
and fork over the $49.99
for one of those puppies
if it was **your** butt
getting wiped
by an ice-cold wipe
six or seven times
a **goddamned** day.

A Piece of Me

Can you explain something to me?
Exactly why
would you want
to keep
the scabby piece of flesh
that came off
during my last diaper change?
It was black.
It smelled.
It was gross.
But you didn't just throw it away.
You kept it.
You put it somewhere safe so you could have it always.
For what reason, I'm at a loss to understand.

I get that you're sentimental.
And that you don't want to miss a moment
of my development.
You'll videotape my first haircut.
You'll put my first scribble in a place of honor on the fridge.
You'll keep the first baby tooth.
>   (Which will actually end up being a mistake when
>   I find it in a few years and you'll have to explain
>   why it isn't with the tooth fairy. Liar.)

I get it.

I really do.

Time is fleeting.

I will grow up.

Memories will fade.

But some things you're just going to have to let go of.

Think of my dried-up bellybutton stump
as a Tibetan Mandala.

Love it, meditate on it, acknowledge its beauty, and then
MOVE ON.

It's temporary.

It's not something to be filed and kept and preserved.

You can cherish it for as long as it's . . .

Oh, never mind.

Moot point.

The cat just ate it.

Nipple Confusion

You didn't give birth to an *idiot*.
I'm not confused.
I just know what I like.

Tummytime

You think this is funny?
Do you like to put turtles on their backs and watch them
struggle to get upright?
You're sadistic,
cruel,
unkind.
You're like the meanest personal trainer in the world.

I was just born.
I can't move.
Cut me some slack.
It's hard enough being on my back.
For the record, just *being* at this point is a slow walk
up a steep hill.

Now flip me back over.
And wait for me
to make the next move.

You Can't Handle the Truth

I have to say,
(and if I could talk, I would)
I find it incredibly amusing
how you pore over books about how to be a better parent.
I see you doing your research,
putting in your time,
making notes in the margins.
You know a tremendous amount
about what to do
and when to do it
and how to do it best.

But it's not working.

I still won't sleep
when you want me to.
I won't stop spitting up
copious quantities of hard-wrought breast milk.
I will cry loudly for long periods
and offer no opening for consolation.
I'm a baby.
It's what I do.
I have my reasons.

And even if I were willing to tell you what they are,
none of them would make sense to you anyway—
Regardless of how many
of the latest
baby care ebooks
you load up
on your fancy
digital
reading
device.

Big Blue Ball

If one were actively looking for a way to torture me,
to make me miserable,
and uncomfortable,
and push me to the brink of insanity,
one couldn't do better than
the nasal aspirator.

I don't *like* being congested,
I'm not gonna say I do,
but I'd rather never be able to breathe
through my nostrils again,
than have you hold me down and
shove that rubber monstrosity up my tender
nasal passages.

I've come to accept the rectal thermometer.
        (You use a lot of lube.)
I'm okay with the nail trimming.
        (When you're not distracted.)
I can even accept the freezing cold wipes
first thing on a winter's morn.
        (At least it wakes me the hell up.)

But that nasal aspirator is the physical manifestation
of everything I loathe and fear and want excised
from my world.
It gives me nightmares.
It never really works.
Plus, it's gross.
And now that I've expressed my feelings on the matter,
if you use it on me again,
I'll have to believe it's less about relieving my congestion
than about your need to create
some emotional distance
between us.

In my crib, **I cry.**
In your bed, **I don't.**

It's not rocket science.

The Conditions of Unconditional Love

It's one thing to name the love between us "unconditional,"
it's another to put that into practice.

I believe that you love me no matter what the conditions,
but you must admit that, under some conditions,
you love me just a little bit less.

I can tell when you're annoyed at me.
You don't hide it very well.
Even if you bite your tongue,
mask your frustration,
take ten deep cleansing breaths,
I'm still aware of your anger.
Your milk tastes mad.

I don't take it personally.
I know how great I am.
You're just in a mood.
It'll pass.
Once you have a nap.

Or something with frosting.
Or I muster up a gesture or facial expression
so freaking adorable
that all is forgiven
and once again,
you remember
to love me
unconditionally.

Same Old, Same Old

The dim lights.
The soft music.
The gentle murmurs.
The massage with lavender oil.

The warm milk.
The fleecy jammies.
The slightly pitchy singing.
The same Boynton book.

Enough already.
This bedtime ritual you've concocted?
It's so *boring*,
a huge yawn.
Dull as dirt.
There's no break in the routine.
Every. Single. Night.
The.
Exact.
Same.
Thing.
I might as well be put to bed by a robot.

But, y'know . . .
maybe you win this one.
'Cause I'd rather sleep
than watch
you
just
go
through
the
motions.

Sometimes I look at you
and I am filled with *love* and *admiration*.

Sometimes I look at you and I'm like,
"Really?"

Giving You What You Need

I may not burp
every time
you feed me.
My body doesn't work that way.
I have to be in the mood.
That's just the way it is.
Yet you refuse to let it go.
You seem really invested
in my producing
some kind of reward
for your effort.
If I don't deliver,
you'll feel like you haven't
done your job.

Okay.
I hate to tell you this . . .
but it's the truth . . .
sometimes . . .
sometimes
I fake it.
I'm sorry.
But if I don't fake it,
you'll just keep

pounding and
pounding and
pounding away at me
until something gives.
(You're very goal oriented.)
But if I make a
convincing
belching sound,
you'll think I'm done,
and then we can move on,
maybe watch a little TV
and go to sleep.

Creative Solutions

Will you get that thing out of my face??!!
What is your problem??!!??
Every time I open my mouth to
express
my
distress,
you try to shove a nipple in it.
Christ, woman, you have got to have
at least **one other color** in your crayon box.
I'm shocked by your lack of inventiveness.
I'm saddened by how willing you are to take
the path of least resistance.
I'm annoyed by your lazy approach to parenting.
And, let me tell you, this is the last time
I'm gonna fall for your . . .
Mmmm. Warm milk.

Who's Right Is Right and Who's Wrong Is . . .

I love Daddy.
I really do.
He's got so many great qualities.
He's funny.
He has a nice singing voice.
He wears soft flannel shirts.
I feel safe in his arms.

But when it comes right down to it . . .
You know that argument you two are constantly having?
The one where you express frustration
about how it feels like you do so much more for me
than he does
and that you're getting less sleep
than he is
and that you're more on top of things
than he is
and that you're, oh, just generally better at everything
than he is?
Guess what?
You're not wrong.

Nope. You're not wrong.
In fact, you're right.
And, you know what else?
It has nothing to do with gender.
A lot of my friends' fathers are their primary caretakers.
Or at least they're responsible for an indisputable
fifty percent.
As I've said, Daddy is great.
Really, really great.
But I'm here to tell you,
as someone who knows,
that it's not even a close race.
Nine times out of ten
(and keep in mind
that I'm really not
that clear on the
whole counting thing yet)
you're the one
whose face I see
appear over my crib
when I cry in the middle of the night.

You're way better
at packing my diaper bag.

You jump up
to get me in the morning.
You have amazing boobs
full of delicious milk.

You're a high standard
by which the poor guy has to measure himself.

I love Daddy.
But that guy has seriously got to step up his game.

The Middle of the Night

My eyes blink open.

I yawn.

I strain to hear a sound.

Nothing.

Nothing but darkness and stillness.

Hmm.

I feel peckish.

I could use a drink,
some company,
kind words.

I make a sound.
No one stirs.
I rustle around in my crib.
Still no response.
Good god, you guys are heavy sleepers.

What does a person have to do to get some service
around here?

Pitch a fit?

Scream one's head off?

Be so loud you get scared I'll wake the neighbors?

Done. Done. And . . . **DONE**.

Well, hello there, Sleepyhead!

Fussy Loves Company

Why are you always on *me* about being **fussy**?
You're **fussy**.

You're **fussy** if you're tired.
You're **fussy** if you're hungry.
You're **fussy** when you have gas.
You're **fussy** when there's nothing on TV.

You're **fussy** when you're too hot or too cold.
You're **fussy** in the morning before caffeine.
You're **fussy** when I wake you up
in the middle of the night.
You're **fussy** when you look in the mirror
and don't like what you see.

You're **fussy** when your mother pays too much
attention to you.
You're **fussy** when your mother doesn't respond
to your call.
You're **fussy** when you're over- and/or under-stimulated.
You're **fussy** sometimes for no apparent reason at all.

The gist is
we're not so different—
you and me.
Clearly, the **fussy** nut
has not fallen far
from its **fussy-ass** tree.

My Window

It's very small.
Tiny, really.
You blink and you miss it.
So don't blink.
Because if you miss my window,
I will make your life miserable.

The window is magic.
I rub my eyes.
I stretch.
I yawn.
If you happen to be on the phone
or in the other room
or on Facebook
when it happens,
there goes the one opportunity I'll give you this morning
for me to go down easy
for a decent nap.

The window opens.
And if you don't shove me through it
and into my crib
and hightail it out of there,

the window will shut
and you and I will have
a good long cranky time together
until that window
is
cracked
open
again.

Attachment Parenting

Honestly,
a little bit of space wouldn't be the worst thing in the world.
You're

always . . .

there.

In my little face.
Up my little butt.

You need to step off.
For just a bit.
So I can breathe.

You read once that
your baby fusses less
when your baby stays close.
And ever since then, I've felt like a joey
in your marsupial pouch.
There's no relief.
I thought being born would mean independence.
I was wrong.

We know that closeness promotes familiarity.
But we also know what familiarity breeds.

The Spice of Life

The world is an amazing place so far.
It's full of beautiful sounds,
psychedelic colors,
fascinating aromas,
an infinite variety of textures
for my uncalloused fingers to feel,
but, um . . . what's with the food here?
So far it's been nothing but something mushy,
room temperature and a bit bland.
I believe I was born with taste buds—
no reason to think I wasn't—
and I'd like to be able to utilize them to their fullest degree.
This can't be it.
It just can't.
And you make all these num-nummy sounds
when you feed me
as if you know how good it tastes
Which it most decidedly DOESN'T.
But when was the last time
you ate whole-grain oatmeal
with breast milk,
uncooked tofu,
puréed peas with no salt
or, for that matter,

mashed banana
or sweet potato
or applesauce.
There has to be more than this.
I have an inkling that there's more to this.
There is just no way that nice Thai man
is delivering a bunch of containers of
this crap to your door twice a week.

Thinking Inside the Box

My first Halloween.
And I'm a . . .
wait for it . . .
this is gonna be good . . .
I come from parents who don't color between the lines . . .
they're willing to take the creative leap . . .
they're untraditional . . .
their creativity knows no bounds . . .
they make the extra effort . . .
go the additional mile . . .
this is going to be fantastic . . .
a Halloween none of us will ever forget . . .
we will be the talk of our neighborhood . . .

Here it is . . .

A pumpkin?!!??

Forgive me for having higher expectations
for you
than that.

Just Go Already

Oh my god.
If I have to listen
to one more day
of your mewing
about not wanting
to go back to work
and have you put it all on **me**
and how hard it's going to be on **me,**
my soft, little baby brain
is going to **explode.**

You have got to stop.
I will be fine.
I like the nanny.
She doesn't make me nap.
She does my hair.
She doesn't make me eat vegetables
before she gives me fruit.
She puts me in a lot of outfits from Tata that she finds
at the bottom of my drawer that, for some reason,
still have the tags on!!

So go.
I'll be fine.
I'll even act extra-specially cute
and happy to see you when you get home
and at least make it *seem*
like your absence
has made my tiny heart
grow
fonder.

First Visit to the Doctor

Are you fucking kidding me?
What the hell is this?
Some stranger is gonna pierce my delicate thigh flesh
with a sharp needle
and inject me with some mysterious fluid
that's gonna sting
and maybe even give me a *FEVER*???
And you call yourself my **parent**!!

Why aren't you protecting me from this?
This is insanity.
Why couldn't I be born to parents
who don't believe in vaccinations?
Why couldn't I have had the luck
to be delivered into that family?
They're the ones who care about their babies.
Those are the ones who nurse them
until they're in preschool.
Those are the ones who endorse the family bed,
who feed on command,
who never say no,
who would rather die
than *Ferberize*.

You shop organic.
You recycle.
You smoke pot occasionally.
You walk around naked.
You don't wax excessively.
But when it comes to vaccinations,
You're a freakin' red state.

Another Lost Sock

In what universe would I keep socks on my feet?
It makes no sense to me.
And, really, if you thought about it clearly
for more than two seconds,
it wouldn't make sense to you either.
I kick,
I pull,
I make a lot of sudden movements.
And sometimes, if I'm feeling particularly annoyed at you,
I'll even push one off deliberately
and watch it meet its new sidewalk home
while you, unaware, briskly push my stroller
right past it
and continue talking
on the cell phone to your friend
Janice.

What the Fuck Is That?

The cat hates me.

You think it's all okay 'cause it doesn't try to scratch
my eyes out.
Or smother me in the night by lying languorously
across my face.
Or bite off one of my vulnerable toes.

But it stares at me
with *scorn.*
And *derision.*
And *loathing.*
It turns its *terrible* gaze on me
and I try to look away, but I'm caught in its
hypnotic glare.

With every highly allergenic fiber of its being,
it focuses its hateful feline energy on me.
It wills me to pull its tail.
It manipulates me into grabbing
a chubby handful of its neck fur.

It exerts some kind of mind control over me
so that when I see it, I giggle and laugh
instead of
scream for my life.

Call me an ailurophobe,
but I'm pretty positive that Petunia is a pyschopomp.

You Cry It Out, Bitches

What is going on?
Everything was fine.
You were nursing me,
cuddling me,
picking me up
when I cried
in the middle
of the night.
But now?
Nothing.

Oh, sorry.
I guess it's not *nothing*.
You do come in and pat my back
WHILE I'M SCREAMING MY LUNGS OUT,
and say, "There. There."
for **two minutes**
and then you're gone.
Well, I've got news for you . . .
That's not comforting, that's just *annoying*.

Oh, I know what this is about!
You're reading that asshole Ferber again, aren't you?
You're trying to get me to self-soothe.

You're shirking your responsibilities
as MY PARENTS.
You're cutting the cord.
AGAIN.

Richard Ferber is a fucking crazy person.
But you listen to him!!
You adhere to his teachings.
You don't sway from his advice.
You might as well be Scientologists.
I'm telling you . . .
the guy is NUTS!

Who would tell a parent *not* to pick up their crying baby?
You don't know
the extent
of my emotional distress.
I can't speak.
I can't tell you what's going on.
I can't articulate the nuances of my emotional journey.
I **can** cry.
Loudly.
For a long time.
That's all I got.

Sure, I'll fall asleep eventually.
And you'll get a good night's sleep
tonight.
I, however, will wear the emotional scars
from this little exercise
in ruthlessness
FOREVER.

But, y'know . . .
if you're okay with that.

I've Never Seen This Man Before in My Life

Whoa.
What the hell is going on here?
Who is this man
and why are you handing me to him
with a huge smile on your face?

It's been my impression thus far
that you're alert to the threat
of nefarious strangers
who might threaten my well-being.
So it seems more than a little odd
that you'd walk up to this man—
this man dressed
in a bright red
polyester
suit
with
a fake beard
and rheumy eyes—
and hand him your *baby*.
And *take photos*
to preserve
the memory
of this event.

This is not for me.
I do not cherish this moment.
In fact,
in the future,
I will only
be able to recall
the experience
when I see
the photograph of myself
red-faced and screaming
on the lap of a man
dressed as a buffoon
who stares expressionless
into the middle distance.

I Won't Dance . . . Don't Ask Me

These "Mommy and **Me**" classes?
The ones that **you** signed **us** up for?
'Cause **you** felt like it was something **we** needed to do?
'Cause everyone else was doing it?
Mmm. Not so much.

Watching **you** dance to the Lollipop song . . .
I wonder if **you** ever had any dignity.
Or, for that matter,
if **you**'ll ever
have any concern
for protecting
mine.

Styling My Self

I'm not happy with my color story.

Just 'cause I don't have a sense of the world at large and its
many nuances doesn't mean I have no sense of fashion.
Just 'cause I have trouble finding my own toes sometimes
doesn't mean that I couldn't pick out a better top to
match my leggings.
Just 'cause I don't know my own name yet
doesn't mean that I don't know that baby blue and aqua
are a tricky combination to pull off.

I realize that baby clothes are expensive.
They won't last long at the rate I grow.
But ya gotta realize that—on some level—
I am representing the family
and how I appear to people—
especially on first impression—
makes a notable difference.
To you.
To me.
(Well, maybe more to you than to me
because everyone knows
I'm not the one

who picked out this
atrocious cabbage-rose-patterned onesie
with ruffles in all the wrong places
and a profoundly unflattering fit.)

Every time you choose an outfit for me,
you need to ask yourself:
"Would I wear this if it came in my size?"
And, if the answer is
"No!! Are you fucking kidding me?"
you need to put that outfit down,
and go find me some
nice black yoga pants,
an asphalt-colored t-shirt
with a slight a-line and three-quarter sleeves
and a pair of black ballet flats.

I'm a baby.
Not a clown.
And only crazy people wear their pajamas
when it's midafternoon.

One of the Annoying Things About You

You know that game we play
pretty much *constantly*?
The one where I put the ball
in the plastic container
(BHA-free of course)
and you dump it out
and give it to me
and I put it back in again?
And you dump it out
and give it to me
and I put it back in *again*?
And you dump it out
and give it to me
and I put it back in **again**?
And you're so freaking amused each time I get the
freaking thing in the stupid container
even though it's really not that hard?
Even for an eleven-month-old?
Right. That's the one.

Well . . .

listen up . . .

COULDJA LEAVE THE FREAKING BALL IN THE CONTAINER?

For once?

I put it there because I want it there.

Just leave it there and let's move on with our lives.

We've got a goddamned game of peek-a-boo to play.

I'm Not Okay

When I bonk myself really, really hard
on the edge of the coffee table . . .
When I fall down 'cause I'm just learning to walk
and I'm still not that steady on my feet . . .
When I slip off the swing 'cause you were checking
your iPhone and not watching me as carefully
as you should have . . .
Guess what?
That shit hurts!!
You've got to know it does.
So why is your first reaction always,
        "You're okay! You're okay!"?
Do you honestly think you're gonna trick me into thinking
I didn't just get an enormous goose egg
on my forehead?
Or that my knee isn't gonna bleed like a motherfucker?
Or that the bruise on my elbow is just a smudge of dirt?
When was the last time *you* smacked a vulnerable part
of *your* anatomy against a hard, unforgiving object?
It HURT, right?
Now imagine everyone around you just dismissing your
pain with an idle wave of the hand

and a pat on the head
and an "Oh, you're okay."
And, even though you actually felt the lump rising on your
head and in your throat, you had to smile gamely through
your discomfort, because you could see that everyone was
just so *invested* in your not crying or making a fuss?
If you understand a fraction of what I'm trying to tell you,
then you understand that "okay" is exactly what I am not.
However . . .
I wouldn't say no to a lollipop.

People Are Strange

Well, of course I **cry** when you **dump** me in the arms of
a **stranger**.
I'm barely even fucking used to you and now you hand me
off to someone new?
I don't like the way this person smells,
> how it holds me,
> the pitch of its voice,
> the cut of its jib.
Who the fuck is this person anyway
and what does it want with me?
It's not aware of my personal space.
It doesn't have boundaries.
It's taking liberties.
It's grinning at me as I cry the tears of someone who's
scared WITLESS!
> **Not cool.**
> And kind of **menacing**.
I really don't care about this person's context.
I have no interest in the years you spent together in the
East Village.
Or the summer you shared a house on a lake in
New Hampshire.

Or the time you got drunk and kissed and you both agreed it was just a silly thing to do, but you find yourself thinking about that kiss more often than you'd want to admit.

It means nothing to me if you trust this person with
your life.
Just don't trust it with
mine.

A Little Space Here?

Not everything I do is so noteworthy.
I'm just trying to live my life over here.
Some things don't come easily to me—
and I appreciate a bit of encouragement—
but the constant patter,
the relentless oohs and aahs over every
minor achievement,
the calling of every play,
that dial could be turned way the fuck down.
Maybe even muted.

I mean, sometimes you just want to . . .
poop
without
it becoming
a goddamned
conversation starter.

Tata & Gampy

Now this is what I'm talkin' about . . .
This is a world I could get used to.

There are no enforced naps.
No food restrictions.
The television is on ALL THE TIME.
And the word "No" is never spoken.
This world is loosey-goosey,
and I embrace its rulelessness.

So what if my diaper gets put on backwards?
So what if choking hazards are always within reach?
So what if I got my first taste of Tanqueray and I'm not yet
twenty months old?
It looked like water, and Gampy can't move
as fast as I can.
I don't mind that I had potato chips and ice cream
for dinner.
I don't care that I was put to bed in my clothes.
It's not a problem that I fell asleep on the floor 'cause it
was **two hours**
past my bedtime.

These people are **REBELS**
and **I LIKE IT.**

You'll get upset at them when you come home
from your date.
You'll marvel at how they ever took care of you as a baby,
how you survived your childhood intact,
but don't think too hard on it.
You're lucky you got free babysitting,
and I'm lucky I made it out of there alive.

Tee(vee)riffic

Isn't she lovely?
Isn't she wonderful?
She's so big and beautiful and hi-def.
When Elmo talks to a baby,
that baby is ME.

From the moment I laid eyes on that
46-inch plasma 1080p high-definition screen,
it was love.
I don't see any reason to look away.
Everything I need is there,
with 65536 colors and crisply delineated focus.
It doesn't get better than this.
Come on . . .
you know what I'm talking about.
Real life doesn't even look this good.
It's certainly not as stimulating.
And I sit and I'm quiet and I watch and I am moved.
And you get to take a shower.
See?
We both win.

Walking a Fine Line

I'm coming to realize
that your self-esteem
is uncomfortably tied up with
when I hit certain milestones.
You want me to walk.
And I'm just not ready.

Crawling gets me where I want to go.
It's fine for now.
An effective means of transport.
I will walk.
It's not like I won't.

Frankly, you were fine with where I was at
until the other night
when your friend called me "Crawl Malden"
and I watched you go over the edge.
I could see the wheels turning.
It became a mission to make me walk
before I (or should I say "we")
could get mocked again.
But it's not really me you're protecting.
I don't feel any pain or humiliation.
This one's about you

and my resistance
to your agenda
is driving you crazy.

You might not have expected
that "resisting your agenda"
would become one of my favorite pastimes
quite so early on
in our relationship,
but then I didn't expect
that your agenda
would be quite so fun to resist.

You're Starting to Scare Me

You know that moment in a thriller
When the hero enters the serial killer's lair
And it's a shrine of snapshots of the next victim?
The walls are covered in pictures.
There's usually a scrapbook . . .

Our home is starting to look like a serial killer lives here
And the next target of his (or her) fixation is me.
This makes me uncomfortable, to say the least.

Over-documentation is the earmark of an obsession
taken too far,
One that can only end very, very badly.

Cease and Desist

Dear Mama and Dada,

It has come to my attention that you have made unauthorized use of my copyrighted work entitled **Anything Cute I Do** (herein known as the "Work") in the preparation of a work derived therefrom. I have reserved all rights in the Work, which was first created on the day I left my mother's uterus.

Your work entitled "My Baby Farts Loudly and Giggles" and which appears on the web at http://www.youtube.com is essentially identical to the Work and clearly used the Work as its basis.

You neither asked for nor received permission to use the Work as the basis for "My Baby Farts Loudly and Giggles" nor to make or distribute copies of it. Therefore, I believe you have willfully infringed my rights under 17 U.S.C. § 101, et seq. and could be liable for statutory damages as high as $100,000 or my weight in Pirate's Booty.[1]

---

1. Currently 100 4-oz. bags, but will be adjusted to correspond to weight at time of delivery of reimbursement for damages.

I demand that you immediately cease the use and distribution of all infringing works derived from the Work, and all copies of it, and that you deliver to me all unused, undistributed copies of it, or destroy such copies immediately, and that you desist from this or any other infringement of my rights in the future. I shall consider taking the full legal remedies available to rectify this situation if I have not received an affirmative response from you indicating that you have fully complied with these requirements by Bedtime.

Sincerely,
Your Baby

Building Our Community

Just because you like that lady with a baby
who's close to my age
does NOT mean
that I am going to like that baby
who's close to my age.
In fact, our chronological age is the only thing I've found to
have in common with that mutant.
It's not like I'm fixing you up with every 37-year-old woman
who walks by
just 'cause she's 37.
I thought I made my feelings clear when I cried
consistently during our play date
(or should I say yours?).
It wasn't my acid reflux.
It was the looks I was getting from Hell-Baby.
And the next get-together?
That block he threw
that landed square
in the middle
of my forehead?
The block that left a *dent*?
No accident.
I have no idea why you were so willing
to give that one a pass.

That baby's a Neanderthal.
That baby's a freak of nature.
That baby is a pain in my goddamned diapered
A+D-ointmented ass.

Look, I'm glad you've found yourself a friend,
Someone who understands what you're going through,
Who has the same concerns, the same experiences . . .
You need a lot of support, validation.
I know that about you.
But I have a request to make.
In the future, I would appreciate not being used as the
means by which you further your own social agenda.
Especially when your social agenda
includes getting a grande soy milk vanilla latte with
a woman whose womb produced the antichrist.

More Fiber in My Diet

I love how you
FREAK OUT
whenever I put a small object in my mouth.
I never see you move so fast.
It's absolutely awesome.
You're like a superhero!!

I know you're protecting me.
I get the whole "choking hazard" concept.
But I can't help it.
What looks like
irresponsible and random
tasting and eating
is actually a
multi-sensory
learning event
involving
sight,
hearing,
touch,
and taste.

I can't just see the small plastic trinket
or hear how it sounds when I throw it at the wall
or feel it's smooth, plasticky goodness with my fingers,
I have to use all my senses to absorb its essence.
That which is not gummed
cannot be said to exist.
(That's either Descartes or Nietzsche.
I always get them confused.)

To What Miserable Wretches Have I Been Born?

You want to know why I won't stop crying?
Why I'm completely inconsolable?
Why my face seems to be stuck in this rictus of despair?
I thought you were smarter than that.
I *hoped* you were smarter than that.
If you need me to spell it out for you
you're shit out of luck,
'cause I don't even know my freaking ABCs.

You **took away the keys** I was playing with.
And, when I started crying hysterically,
you tried to give them back.
But now it's too late.
What's done is done.
You can't turn back time.
Forget the keys!!!
It was never about them anyway.
Don't you see?
It was all a test. A test!
And you failed.

Oh, damn it all to hell.
I don't care about those trinkets anymore.
I only care about your neglect
and your inability
to meet my needs and—
let's not mince words—
your complete inadequacy as parents.

On a Short Leash

If you're thinking of getting me one of those
leashes,
harnesses,
safety restraints,
cute plush-y animal backpacks
with a long plush-y tether . . .

stop.

Suck It

Can you explain to me
what makes you
so very uncomfortable
with my pacifier?

I like to suck.
You taught me that.
I got rewarded for sucking.
I got fed. With warm, delicious milk.
I felt close to you.
Heck . . . I felt close to achieving Nirvana.
Can you blame me for wanting to keep that sense of
peace and oneness going for just a little longer?

Sucking on something makes me feel like I might
have a chance at being a truly successful human being.
Can you say that about any of your vices?
You wish you could find something that makes you feel
this good about life.
Something that wasn't bad for you . . .
didn't rot your liver,
give you cancer,
slow down your brain.

Just clean, honest impulse satisfaction.
It's hurting no one.
Except maybe you and your fragile sense
of confident parenting
in the face of some random stranger's perceived judgment
while
on line
at
CVS.

iConfess

iHave
to
say
that
sometimes
iLove
your
iPhone
more
than
iLove
you.

iSorry.

My Feelings About My Feelings

I know you're really sad that we can't go
outside right now.

Oh, really, Einstein?
What's tipping you off?
The high-pitched screaming?
The tears rolling down my cheeks?
The stamping of my feet?
The throwing of toys?
"Sad" doesn't cut it.
Try "devastated" and "wrecked."

Mommy and Daddy understand
that you're frustrated.

Uh-huh.
So you're saying you understand my frustration,
but you're not willing to relieve it?
Guess what that does for me?
MAKES ME MORE FUCKING FRUSTRATED,
THAT'S WHAT!
Whatever gave you the idea that this was helpful?

Oooh. You're very mad, aren't you?

Don't patronize me.
I am well aware of my anger.
I'm not in control of it, but I'm *aware* of it.
I'm expressing it the only way I know how.
And your calling a spade a spade does nothing for me.

I understand my emotions perfectly well.
You don't need to label them for me.
Especially not with insufficient
and inadequate words
that only remotely indicate
the scope and depth of
my feelings.
You better get yourself a thesaurus,
because, baby, I've been holding back.
This isn't the worst I've got.
In fact, you ain't seen nuthin' yet.
You're not gonna be able to name
the feelings I got waiting in the wings.

The Sounds of Being Humiliated

"What's the doggie say?"
    Oof. Ooof.
"What's the kitty say?"
    Me-owww.
"What's the rooster say?"
    Ack-a-doodle-doo.
"What's the lion say?"
    Rawr.
"What's the pig say?"
    Oink. Oink.
"What's the horsie say?"
    Nay-ay-ay.

Okay.
Enough.
I'm out.
I'm done.
I'm bored.
I am not your puppet.
I am not your clown.
I am *not* your trained monkey.

    Eee-eee-eee.

Me Do

There's only one goal parents need to have:
To foster a healthy sense of independence
in their offspring.

It's well documented in the animal kingdom.
> Hawks teach their eyases to hunt small rodents.
> Orcas teach their calves to surface to breathe.
> Otters teach their pups to use rocks to open shellfish.
> Foxes teach their kits to be foxy.

I'm sure you have this *idea* that you're encouraging
my growth as a self-sufficient being,
But the truth is, you're really holding me back.
You get frustrated
whenever I try to do anything by myself.
You're openly annoyed
when I try to feed myself.
You judge me
when I pick out my clothes by myself.
You won't let me
push my own stroller as often as I'd like.
And, god forbid, I try to call a friend on your iPhone.

I really don't know
what confounds you
about my persistence.
I've inherited your eyes,
your hair,
your nail beds.
Why wouldn't I inherit
your obsessive need to control?

NO

NO is just a word.

You say **NO** all the time.
Why can't I say **NO**, too?
I have opinions.
Some are negatively inclined.
And sometimes you ask me questions
to which the appropriate answer is **NO**.

I live in a house of hypocrisy
where different rules apply
for those who have a larger vocabulary
and more advanced motor control.

You wanted me to learn to talk.
But you're not interested in what I have to say
when what I have to say is **NO**.

The irony
is that eventually you're going to view
my commitment to the clear expression of my needs
as a *good* thing.
But, right now,
you're really fucking
with my freedom of speech.

A Battle of Wills

You're standing there
Watching me try to get my rain boots on.

I struggle to shove my foot
Into the rubber boot
And it's not working
And you're not doing *anything* to help.

Oh. I get it.
You want me to learn
how to deal
with my frustration and
strategize my way *rationally*
through this fine motor skill snafu.

> *Healthy doses of frustration*
> *help a child have just the right amount*
> *of resistance to keep him reaching*
> *for his fullest potential.*

All right already.
I get it.
Now can you just help me get the fucking boot on?
I promise I'll reach for my full potential tomorrow.

By the way,
I've also been doing my research.

> *Be sure you model the healthy way*
> *to handle frustration for your child.*

You think I haven't seen how you get
when you reach your limit?
The way you freak out
when the Wi-Fi connection's down?
The way you tear apart
your bedroom looking for
something to wear
out to dinner with friends
that doesn't make you feel
like a chunky monkey?
The way you fly into a rage
when you realize that
the DVR deleted
the most recent episode
of *Project Runway*
and you were all set
for a night
in front of the television
watching them
"make it work."

In those situations,
I'm here to tell you,
you're not such a model
of calm collectedness yourself,
girlfriend.

You What??!!??

Are you freaking kidding me??!!??
You took apart my crib?
My crib???!!
And now it's in pieces?
In the closet?
All because I spent one night—
ONE NIGHT!!!—
In my "Big-Girl Bed" without complaint?
So what if I seemed perfectly happy and content
to make the change?
That was *yesterday.*
Today is another day and
I want my fucking crib back!
Get your ass over to your computer,
call up the assembly instructions on the Internet—
grab a fucking screwdriver and a goddamned wrench and
PUT THE DAMN THING BACK TOGETHER!!

Oh.
Uh-huh.
I see how this is gonna be.
I'm starting to get the picture.
I am not allowed to change my mind.

If I say something—*anything*—I better be able to
follow through.
There is no turning back in this household,
so one better be damned sure
of what one is
endorsing or rejecting
at any given moment
'cause that shit is written in stone.

Oh, oh, that I could have my crib back.
I would stare at you contemptuously through the bars
remaining silent for fear of being misinterpreted
or be held prisoner by my words.
My crib, formerly a place of security and comfort,
would become the physical representation of
the emotional and spiritual confinement
that pervades our home.

Oh, and P.S.: **I WANT MY FUCKING CRIB BACK!!!**

All in Good Time

I think this is one of those situations
where we may
just have to
agree to disagree.

You like to use the potty.
I enjoy my diaper.
It's really a matter of personal preference.
I just don't see how your way is superior.

I feel like this is yet another example of
your dogged unwillingness to see
things from my point of view.
I don't like arguing with you,
but you're not gonna win this one.
'Cause watching
the machinations
you'll put yourself through
to stage manage
where and when
I void my bowels
is completely entertaining.

This one's really important to you.
I can see that.
And if I were a nicer human being,
I'd do what I could to alleviate your anxiety
About guiding me through this
crucial moment in my physical and emotional
development.
But I'm not.
Nicer.
'Cause get this . . .
I know *how* to use the potty.
I just don't *want* to.

Meaningful Consultation

In what universe would I be okay with you
bringing another baby into this house?
You already have a baby . . . ME!!
And I'm not done being your only baby yet.
I am sorry about your advanced maternal age
and the decreasing viability of your ovum,
but that is not my problem!
You should've planned better.
You should've settled on that guy you dated
before you started dating Dad.
He was perfectly fine.
There was nothing wrong with him.
And then you could've started procreating years ago
and I would've been in kindergarten or at least pre-K
and this wouldn't have been quite so disruptive to the
lifestyle to which I've become accustomed.
You know, the one **you** got me accustomed to . . .
The one where **I AM THE ONLY BABY.**
The one where you respond to my needs *immediately*
'cause there's nothing else distracting you.
That's the life I signed up for.
That's the routine I was settling into.
That's the nest I'm not ready to be pushed out of.

Did anyone ever ask me what I wanted?
No.
I'm just supposed to accept this
dramatic change
to my daily existence
in return for what?
A Melissa and Doug Deluxe Wooden Folding Castle.
Whatev.
You'll get yours.
When you're living
in a house with not one,
but *two*

TEENAGERS.

Acknowledgments

First off, I'd like to acknowledge my editor, Greer Hendricks, for getting the humor in this book instantly. From our first conversation when she conveyed her enthusiasm and joy about these poems to our most recent one this morning when she told me to get off my lazy ass and get the acknowledgments done today ("I'm not kidding, Suzanne. TODAY."), she has been a source of limitless support and encouragement.

My literary agent, Daniel Greenberg, is a master at finding the right home for my books. I mean, I know that's what he's supposed to be good at, but he happens to be exceptionally good at it. And I appreciate him for it.

Judith Curr, my publisher, is enormously involved and helpful. She is a true publishing visionary, and I am thrilled to have been invited into her exclusive club of bestselling authors (sometimes if I write things, I think I will make them true . . .).

Thanks to Sarah Cantin, my editor's right-hand woman, who has dealt with my questions, concerns, and demands efficiently and with grace. (Although who knows what facial expressions she's making on the other end of the phone. Might be best to move future communications to iChat.)

I'm grateful to Alan Dingman for designing the cover and drawing that baby. I have stared at that baby like it's my own baby. And I love that baby just like it's my own baby. Also, thanks to Jeanne Lee, who knew Alan was the right man for the job, and to Kyoko Watanabe, who did a lovely job designing the interior of this book.

Diana Franco and the rest of the Atria family have all been terrific so far. But it's early. If this book is a smash hit and goes into several additional printings, then I'll make sure to give everybody an even bigger thank-you in the next edition. Well, let's just go ahead and count on that.

I'd like to thank Dan Brecher for never wavering in his support of me. If anyone knew how emotionally present and thoughtful and warm he actually is, Dan's reputation as a soulless Hollywood agent would be completely compromised. Oops.

Crissy Guerrero was my audience of one on a drive back to LA from a weekend in Palm Springs. Her heartfelt laughter was the fuel I needed to turn the first few poems into a book proposal. Arielle Eckstut, Elizabeth Hannan, Chris Mellon, Neeltje Henneman, and Janice Maloney contributed suggestions, ideas, and support throughout the writing process. (By the way, I have a lot of other friends, but they didn't really do anything to help with this book, so I'm not gonna acknowledge them here.)

Now that I've finally come out behind the curtain as Suzanne Weber, I can actually thank my parents, Idelle and Julian Weber. I was fortunate to have been born to people who made having a sense of humor a priority. I know my father would have loved this book. So much of what I write is to make him laugh. The fact that he's gone hasn't really changed that.

How do you even begin to thank someone like my husband, @DuvaChristopher, who is just hands-down the best human being in every possible way imaginable? You can't. You can just acknowledge how ridiculously lucky you are to have found him. And I do.

I'd also like to thank the babies who inspired poems: Lucy, Gordon, Sophie, Nick, Rebecca, Easton, Lena, Violet, Hudson, and, of course, my own sweet Julia.

Printed in the United States
By Bookmasters